100% UNOFFICIAL

FORTNITE

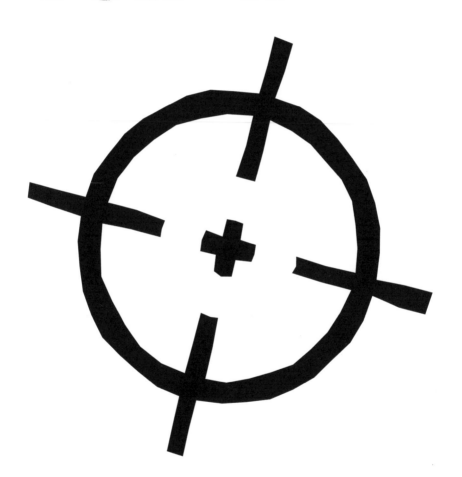

ESSENTIAL GUIDE

Brimming with creative inspiration, how-to projects, and useful information to enrich your everyday life, Quarto Knows is a favorite destination for those pursuing their interests and passions. Visit our site and dig deeper with our books into your area of interest: Quarto Creates, Quarto Cooks, Quarto Homes, Quarto Lives, Quarto Drives, Quarto Explores, Quarto Gifts, or Quarto Kids.

Inspiring | Educating | Creating | Entertaining

First published in 2018 by Dean, an imprint of Egmont UK Limited. Published in the US by becker&mayer books, an imprint of The Quarto Group, 11120 NE 33rd Place, Suite 201, Bellevue, WA 98004 USA. **www.QuartoKnows.com**

becker&mayer! books titles titles are also available at discount for retail, wholesale, promotional, and bulk purchase. For details, contact the Special Sales Manager by email at specialsales@quarto.com or by mail at The Quarto Group, Attn: Special Sales Manager, 100 Cummings Center Suite 265D, Beverly, MA 01915 USA.

19 20 21 22 23 5 4 3 2 1

ISBN: 978-0-7603-6576-2

Library of Congress Cataloging-in-Publication Data available upon request.
Design: Joe Bolder
Editorial: Neil Kelly

Printed, manufactured, and assembled in Italy, 12/18

MIX
Paper from
responsible sources
FSC
www.fsc.org   FSC® C005461

#327311

100% UNOFFICIAL

FORTNITE

ESSENTIAL GUIDE

CONTENTS

INTRODUCTION

HELLO, AND WELCOME ...

... to this totally unofficial, essential guide to playing *Fortnite*, the game that has **LITERALLY** taken the world–and millions of players–by storm. Everyone from rappers and athletes to movie stars and pro-gamers are totally into *Fortnite*'s "Battle Royale" mode. And here's why: it's all about the **ACTION**! In each game, 100 players jump out of a flying "Battle Bus" and glide down onto a mysterious island. In a full-on fight for survival, players shoot it out, eliminating each other in fast-moving skirmishes. The last person standing is the winner, claiming a hard-earned "Victory Royale"!

Like other Battle Royale-style games, *Fortnite* features a **HUGE** map to explore. There are loads of loot-filled chests to discover and an advancing, deadly, player-zapping storm wall keeps gamers on their toes. Landing on the island with nothing but a pickaxe, you'll need to seek out weapons, harvest building materials, and loot everything from healing potions and damage traps to rocket launchers and portable campfires.

You'll build forts and bases, encounter loot-packed supply llamas, race around in all-terrain karts (ATKs), and–if you feel like it–you can even teleport through rifts in the fabric of the universe! On top of that, there are a host of **CRAZY** outfits to wear, from superhero-style costumes to teddy-bear suits. There's also dancing ... yes, you read that right, dancing. From the Floss and the Dab to Groove Jam and the Wiggle, you can bust your best moves with *Fortnite*'s cool "emotes"!

If you're a **NOOB** playing for the first time, or if you just want to improve your *Fortnite* skills, everything you need to know can be found here. Chock-full of hints and tips, this book is packed with useful advice, based on hours of gameplay and the lessons learned from making **TONS** of mistakes! We'll teach you how to use your tools, weapons, and equipment to survive and–most importantly–how to **WIN** and claim your own Victory Royales.

Good luck–see you out there on the battlefield!

The 100% UNOFFICIAL FORTNITE ESSENTIAL GUIDE team

GAME EDITIONS

Ready for your first game? It's time to make a choice, as there are a few options you'll need to decide on before you board the Battle Bus. These pages will help you choose which gaming platform suits you best and whether to go into battle alone, team up with a partner, or join a squad.

WHICH PLATFORM?

Fortnite can be played on PCs, Apple Macs, gaming consoles, and several mobile devices. The quality of the graphics varies a bit, but they all play pretty much the same. With the game's **MASSIVE** global appeal, it should soon be available on even more screens!

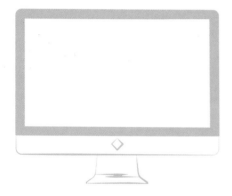

COMPUTER (DESKTOP & LAPTOP)
• PC: Windows 7/8/10 64-bit
• Apple Mac: macOS Sierra and above

CONSOLES
• Xbox One   • PlayStation 4
• Xbox One X   • PlayStation 4 Pro
• Nintendo Switch

DID YOU KNOW?
It's easy to team up with a friend for a game of Fortnite, even if they use a different type of platform–a computer, console, or mobile device–than you. Using the Party Finder option on the main menu, you can "cross-play" by searching for your Epic Friends on other devices. To do this, you must have an Epic Games account!

MOBILE
• iPhone: iOS 11
• iPad mini 4/Air 2 and above
• Android (coming soon ...)

SAVE THE WORLD OR BATTLE ROYALE?

After you've selected a platform, you'll need to choose a game mode–Save the World or Battle Royale. This book focuses **EXCLUSIVELY** on *Fortnite*'s Battle Royale mode.

Save the World is the original *Fortnite* mode. It's an exciting co-op adventure you can play online with friends or alongside computer-generated teammates. There's also a solo gameplay option. In a randomly generated map, you must fight to survive, protecting your base from monsters known as husks.

Battle Royale is a 100 player-versus-player (PvP) survival game. In this free-to-play *Fortnite* mode, gamers battle it out with the objective of eliminating or evading their foes; the last survivor is the winner. Players must also stay within a shrinking safe zone; outside it, a lethal, advancing storm wall inflicts fatal damage.

BATTLE ROYALE MODES

In Battle Royale, you select between three main gameplay modes. Check them all out, as they focus on different gameplay aspects and offer varying levels of difficulty. Temporary limited edition modes are also featured regularly.

SOLO

In Solo mode, you'll single-handedly take on 99 foes, all of whom are out to eliminate you and win. To survive, you'll need to loot, build and take out your enemies before they get you in their crosshairs!

DUOS

Fancy teaming up with a partner? In Duos mode, you can join forces with a pal and work together to eliminate the opposition. Plus, a partner can also revive you if you're wounded.

SQUADS

If you want to be part of a large team, choose Squads mode. You can split into sub-teams to take control of different areas, or stay together in one unit. This is probably *Fortnite*'s most popular mode.

CONTROLS

After you've chosen a gaming platform, you'll need to master *Fortnite*'s basic controls. These pages are a handy guide that you can refer back to at any time. Familiarizing yourself with the controls from the start will really help to build up your speed and improve every aspect of your gameplay. Trust us!

PC AND MAC CONTROLS

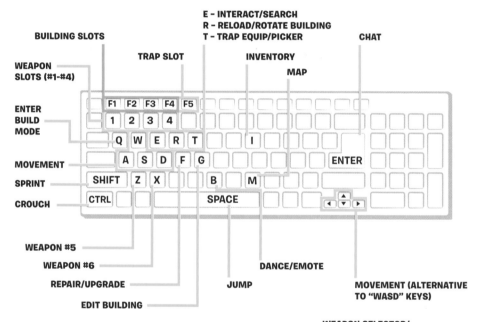

E – INTERACT/SEARCH
R – RELOAD/ROTATE BUILDING
T – TRAP EQUIP/PICKER

BUILDING SLOTS

CHAT

TRAP SLOT

INVENTORY

WEAPON
SLOTS (#1-#4)

MAP

ENTER
BUILD
MODE

MOVEMENT

SPRINT

CROUCH

WEAPON #5

WEAPON #6

REPAIR/UPGRADE

EDIT BUILDING

DANCE/EMOTE

JUMP

MOVEMENT (ALTERNATIVE
TO "WASD" KEYS)

WEAPON SELECTOR/
BUILDING PIECE SELECTOR

SHOOT/CONFIRM CRAFTING/RESURRECT

AIM (ZOOM IN)/
CHANGE BUILDING
MATERIAL

DID YOU KNOW?

If you don't want to use the set-up shown here, you can customize the controls to suit your own style of play. Go to the Settings menu to create your own key combinations. Top Fortnite players often use personalized set-ups that increase their speed, especially in building–so why not look online to check out the controls used by the pros!

MOBILE CONTROLS

TAP TO AIM

TAP TO OPEN MAP

DRAG ANYWHERE TO AIM/
TAP ANYWHERE TO FIRE
WEAPON

OPEN EMOTES

TAP TO CROUCH

TAP TO FIRE

OPEN MENU

TAP TO RELOAD

TAP TO JUMP

DRAG TO MOVE/
DOUBLE TAP TO
AUTO RUN

TAP TO OPEN
INVENTORY

TAP TO SELECT

ENTER BUILD MODE

NINTENDO SWITCH

One of the latest additions to *Fortnite*'s gaming platforms, the Nintendo Switch offers players the best of both worlds. You can battle it out console-style at home, connected to your TV, or shoot it out on the go in mobile mode!

XBOX ONE CONTROLS

Our favorite controller layout is *Fortnite*'s Builder Pro configuration. Here are the must-know functions ...

COMBAT

AIM DOWN SIGHTS (LT)

MAP

ATTACK/CONFIRM (RT)

PREVIOUS WEAPON (LB)

GAME MENU

NEXT WEAPON (RB)

RELOAD/
INTERACT

HARVESTING TOOL

MOVEMENT
(DOUBLE-CLICK
TO SPRINT)

ENTER BUILD MODE/
EDIT BUILD (HOLD)

INVENTORY

JUMP

LOOK/
CROUCH (TAP)/
REPAIR (HOLD)

SQUAD COMMS

EMOTE

BUILDING

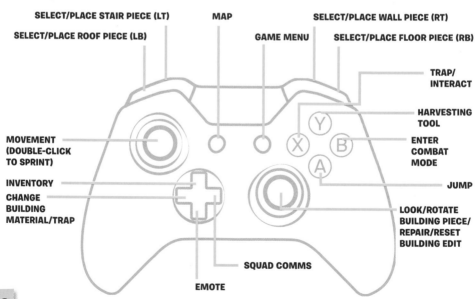

SELECT/PLACE STAIR PIECE (LT)

MAP

SELECT/PLACE WALL PIECE (RT)

SELECT/PLACE ROOF PIECE (LB)

GAME MENU

SELECT/PLACE FLOOR PIECE (RB)

TRAP/
INTERACT

HARVESTING
TOOL

MOVEMENT
(DOUBLE-CLICK
TO SPRINT)

ENTER
COMBAT
MODE

INVENTORY

JUMP

CHANGE
BUILDING
MATERIAL/TRAP

LOOK/ROTATE
BUILDING PIECE/
REPAIR/RESET
BUILDING EDIT

SQUAD COMMS

EMOTE

PLAYSTATION 4 CONTROLS

COMBAT

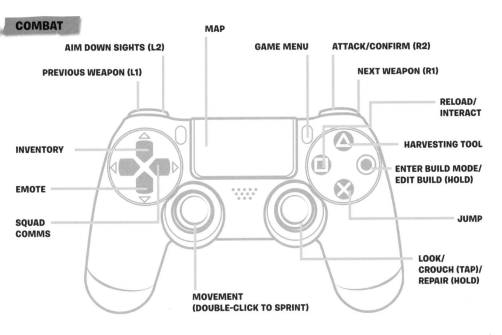

AIM DOWN SIGHTS (L2)

MAP

GAME MENU

ATTACK/CONFIRM (R2)

PREVIOUS WEAPON (L1)

NEXT WEAPON (R1)

RELOAD/
INTERACT

INVENTORY

HARVESTING TOOL

EMOTE

ENTER BUILD MODE/
EDIT BUILD (HOLD)

SQUAD
COMMS

JUMP

LOOK/
CROUCH (TAP)/
REPAIR (HOLD)

MOVEMENT
(DOUBLE-CLICK TO SPRINT)

BUILDING

SELECT/PLACE STAIR PIECE (L2)

MAP

GAME MENU

SELECT/PLACE WALL PIECE (R2)

SELECT/PLACE ROOF PIECE (L1)

SELECT/PLACE FLOOR PIECE (R1)

TRAP/
INTERACT

INVENTORY

HARVESTING TOOL

SQUAD COMMS

CHANGE
BUILDING
MATERIAL/
TRAP

ENTER COMBAT
MODE

JUMP

LOOK/ROTATE
BUILDING PIECE/
REPAIR/RESET
BUILDING EDIT

EMOTE

MOVEMENT
(DOUBLE-CLICK TO SPRINT)

11

ESSENTIAL TIPS FOR NOOBS

The great thing about *Fortnite* is that you can pick it up and play right away! This book will show you how to master the methods that will help you to win a Victory Royale, but here's how to jump straight into the action!

PREPARING FOR BATTLE ...

1 **CHOOSE YOUR MODE**
On the Lobby screen you can decide which game mode you're going to play. There are different styles of match, but your first decision is whether to play alone, as one half of a duo, or as part of a larger squad of up to 50 other players!

2 **VOLUME CONTROL**
Whether you're playing alone or in a team, headphones will greatly improve your gameplay. You'll be able to communicate with your squad, sense enemies approaching and hear the sound of hidden golden loot chests.

3 **BIRD'S-EYE VIEW**
After a short spell on "Spawn Island" (during which time you can familiarize yourself with the controls) you'll find yourself aboard the Battle Bus. From here you can see the entire main island, so decide where you want to land and wait for the perfect time to free fall into the action!

REGISTER AN ACCOUNT

To be able to play *Fortnite*, you need to have an Epic Games account. Registering is a quick process, needing only your name, a display name (avoid using your real name–go with something cool), your email address, and a password. After you've created an account, you can log in. You MUST agree to the End User License Agreement, so get a parent or guardian's permission.

4 HARVEST AND BUILD

When you touch down on the map you'll be holding your axe. So get to it! Trees, buildings, rocks ... swing at them all to harvest the materials you need to get building! Practice makes perfect, so build whenever you get the time and opportunity.

5 EXPLORE THE ISLAND

It doesn't matter where you land on the map, the chances are you'll find weapons and golden chests nearby. Thoroughly search the area around you and grab anything that's useful.

6 KEEP AN EYE ON THE STORM

The storm may be terrifying but it's also quite predictable. Keep an eye on your map during the first moments of the match, as it'll soon show the most direct route to the safe zone. Don't rush–keep an eye on the countdown and you'll be fine.

7 NOT ARMED, NOT DANGEROUS

One of the first things you need is a weapon. More often than not, you will land close to other players and they'll be after you. If they find you before you manage to get your hands on a weapon, it will be almost impossible to defend yourself. Be armed!

8 GETTING ORGANIZED

One press of a button will let you organize your inventory. There's no correct way to do it, but we go with our fave weapons first, and bandages or shields last. Practice switching between them to save valuable time in critical moments. Switching is quicker than reloading ...

USING THE LOBBY

Once you're set up with your very own Epic Games account, you'll be directed to the Lobby screen. Here, you'll find gameplay mode settings, daily challenges, progress displays, and much more. After you've checked out the on-screen info, you'll be ready for your first Battle Royale. **LOCK AND LOAD!**

SEASON BOX

In every *Fortnite* Season, you acquire Experience Points (XP) and advance through Season Levels. XP are earned by competing in matches and taking on daily challenges. When you level up, you gain Battle Stars. This box shows your Season Level, how many XP you have, and how many you need to reach the next Level. At the launch of a new Season, your Season Level resets.

PASS TIERS

This indicates what Tier you are currently on in the Battle Pass (or Free Pass) system. To advance a Tier, you'll need ten Battle Stars. The display tells you the number of Stars required to move up. As you progress through the Tiers, more rewards will be unlocked.

DAILY CHALLENGES

Fortnite's daily challenges keep players coming back, day after day! Examples include taking out foes with an assault rifle or finishing in the Top 6 in Squads mode. This box tells you how many times you need to complete the challenge and the amount of XP and Battle Stars you'll receive if you do so. Battle Stars help you move up Tiers, earning you rewards.

SQUAD SLOTS

There are four squad "slots"—one for each of the four team members (including yourself) in Squads mode. To team up with friends, click on an empty squad slot and scroll through your Epic Friends list. When you've found your pal, send an invite and they'll appear in the selected slot when they accept.

V-BUCKS & FRIENDS

These two panels show you how many V-Bucks you have left to spend (we'll discuss V-Bucks on page 20) and how many of your Epic Friends are currently online, and therefore available to team up with you in a squad or duo.

SETTINGS MENU

This button takes you to the Settings menu, where you can tweak your audio/visual preferences, including switching off audio chat. You can also customize your controls settings, alter your privacy settings, and manage your Epic Friends across multiple platforms and devices.

DID YOU KNOW?

You can take out two enemies at once in Duos mode! When an enemy turns up to revive their wounded partner, line them **BOTH** up in your sights and let rip with your guns. **BOOM!**

MATCH TYPE

Select the mode—Solo, Duos or Squads—here. You may also find temporary limited edition modes; some are only around for a few days! You can choose "Fill" or "Don't Fill" to build a team, but if you select "Don't Fill" you won't be teamed up. By selecting "Fill," you'll be randomly paired up or given three random teammates by *Fortnite*'s matchmaking system.

PRO TIP

If you **MUST** have a full-on challenge, or are playing with pals, choose "Don't Fill". If not, always go for the "Fill" option (see Match Type). The worst case scenario is that randoms will be useless. On the positive side, they could just help you to **WIN!**

ITEM SHOP CAREER STORE

300 + 0

FRIEND LINK

NEW MODE AVAILABLE!

50 V 50
SQUADS
FILL

PLAY

Inspect Challenges Emote News

NEWS BUTTON

Press this to find out Epic Games' latest news, including game updates, new modes, weapons, emotes, and more.

PLAY BUTTON

Hitting the "Play" button transports you to "Spawn Island." While you wait for the Battle Bus to take you to the battlefield, you can loot, shoot, build, run around and dance! You won't be here long and your activities won't earn you rewards or affect gameplay. Use this time to practice building structures and tracking your foes.

PASSES & CHALLENGES

In *Fortnite*, you have access to two types of pass—the Free Pass and the Battle Pass, which are refreshed and replaced every Season. You'll have to pay to acquire the Battle Pass, but both types will reward you with loot as you advance. The rewards won't improve your skills, but they will make you look super-cool!

PASS PROGRESSION

No matter which Pass you have, the free or paid variety, you'll advance in the game by collecting Battle Stars and raising your rank via the Tier system. You can see all the available rewards at each Tier from the Battle Pass tab of the Home screen.

CLIMBING TIERS

Every Pass is split up into numbered Tiers, each of which may reward you with a certain type of loot, from awesome emotes to cool items like skins, contrails, and even some extra V-Bucks! To progress from Tier to Tier, you'll need to earn Battle Stars. Your Tier level is displayed at the top-left corner of the Battle Pass screen, and you can see which rewards you've earned by looking for the green tick icon over items.

BATTLE STARS

You'll need to get Battle Stars to advance through the Battle Pass and Free Pass. Doing challenges is the speediest way to acquire them. Five Battle Stars can be collected by completing daily challenges; weekly ones can earn you even more. You'll also pick up Battle Stars by leveling up your Season Level as you gain more XP.

WEEKLY CHALLENGES

In the Battle Pass, players can take on weekly challenges. New challenges are unlocked each week. Like the daily challenges, an on-screen display shows you the number of times you'll need to complete a task to win the challenge, and the reward you'll receive. Completing a whole week of challenges will earn you **LOADS** of XP. If you've started playing late in the Season, or don't want to shell out for the Battle Pass, there are also a host of challenges to complete for the Free Pass.

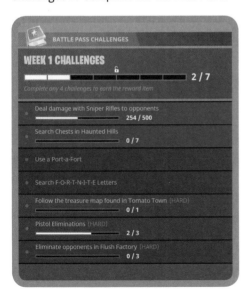

CLIMB TIERS QUICKLY

- **MASTER THIEF** – Start earning XP without firing a shot; loot ammo crates, golden chests, and supply drops to boost your level instead.

- **REACH THE TOP** – Achieving a higher finishing position will reward you with more XP. Be smart about it—hide within the safe circle and only engage when necessary to make it to a respectable position.

- **TAKE THEM OUT** – Track down enemies, get as close as possible and fire away. Each elimination will reward you with a bunch of XP.

- **PURCHASE THE BATTLE PASS** – All your hard work could be more greatly rewarded by opting for the paid Battle Pass. XP earnings will be boosted for the entire Season.

- **SQUAD GOALS** – Team up with friends in Squads or Duos—for every member in your squad that has a Battle Pass, you'll get a 10% XP bonus, which means a 40% boost playing Squads.

FILLING YOUR LOCKER

Wondering where your **SUPER-COOL** outfits and equipment are stored? You'll find them in your Locker—all the gear that you've earned through your Battle Pass or purchased from the Item Shop is kept on this screen. None of it will help you to win a Victory Royale, but you'll look good trying!

BANNER

Clicking on the banner slot in the Lobby screen enables you to edit your personal banner. Customize it by choosing from a range of shapes, including pickaxes, rockets, bombs, stars, llamas, and more. There are 21 colors to choose from and you click to apply them. You can acquire loads more awesome banner icons by leveling up and advancing in the Battle Pass.

OUTFITS

Fight it out in style on the battlefield! There are lots of amazing outfits to choose from, and you can earn them from the Battle Pass or purchase them in the Item Shop. Once they're here in the Locker, they're yours forever.

BACK BLING

As the name suggests, these blingy, fashionable items, such as capes, wings, and backpacks, are worn on the back of your battle outfits. Back bling is earned through progress in the Battle Pass, but you'll also acquire them as extra freebies when you buy specific outfits at the Item Shop.

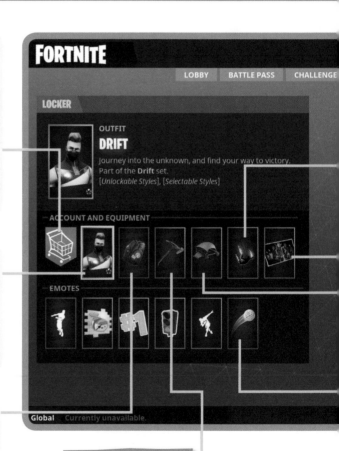

HARVESTING TOOLS

When you begin a game of *Fortnite*, you're given a standard pickaxe to harvest wood, brick, and metal for fort-building. If you fancy a change, build up a collection of harvesting tools and store them here. They can be acquired through the Battle Pass or by shelling out V-Bucks in the Item Shop.

EMOTES

You can assign up to six emotes for a game of *Fortnite*, to express yourself through dances and gestures. The Free Pass features one standard emote; you can pick up more, like the three shown here, in the Battle Pass or Item Shop.

GROOVE JAM **DANCE MOVES** **WIGGLE**

| 300 | + | 0 |

ITEM SHOP   **CAREER**   **STORE**

CONTRAILS

A contrail is a special visual effect that appears around your *Fortnite* character as you skydive from the flying Battle Bus towards the island. Fall in style by choosing a contrail from here to display as you plummet into battle! At present, the Battle Pass is the only way to get new contrails.

LOADING SCREENS

It's possible to choose the screens that appear while *Fortnite* loads on your PC, Mac, or mobile device. They can all be stored in your Locker. Collecting screens may not be as exciting as acquiring outfits, back bling, and toys, but you can get them by moving up the Tiers through the Battle Pass.

GLIDERS

Touch down in style on the battlefield with one of *Fortnite*'s wicked gliders. There are lots to choose from—the Viking llama boat is our current fave! Like all items in your Locker, you can pick up new gliders by handing over V-Bucks or progressing through Tiers in the Battle Pass.

TOYS

You can now earn basketballs, beach balls, golf balls and more through the Battle Pass. In Lazy Links, it's possible to play a complete round of golf! Equipped in the emote slots, toys can be used in a game for fun but they won't help you to secure Victory Royales.

ITEM SHOP & CAREER SCREEN

It's time to fill your Locker up with tons of awesome things! If you have a Battle Pass, you'll earn rewards as you progress. But if you want to splurge those V-Bucks, the Item Shop has loads of cool items for you to stash away. If you see something you like, grab it—it may not be there for long!

ITEM SHOP & V-BUCKS

SHOP SWAG

In the Item Shop, you'll find "limited-time" goodies such as gliders, outfits, and emotes, which are only available to buy for a short time. There are also "Featured Items," which are often linked. For example, you may be able to purchase a matching outfit and glider or a paired outfit and harvesting tool. Item Shop gear is changed regularly and some items may **NEVER** reappear! But once you've bought your cool swag, it's yours for keeps.

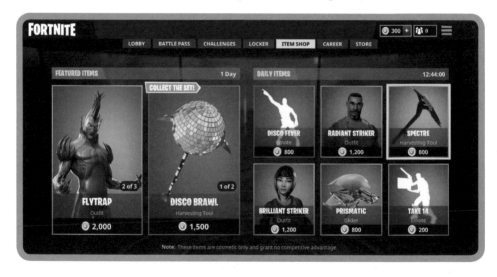

WHAT ARE V-BUCKS?

If you want to buy stuff from the Item Shop, you'll need to use V-Bucks, *Fortnite*'s in-game currency. They can only be bought in batches, such as 1,000, 2,500, 6,000, and so on. To get V-Bucks, you'll need to purchase them using real money on the Store page. V-Bucks can also be earned by advancing through Tiers in your Battle Pass.

CAREER SCREEN

USING THE CAREER SCREEN

Check out this screen to find your profile, which displays all your game stats. You can also take a look at the leaderboards; by toggling between your friends you can discover who's the best player in your group—and who's the biggest **LOSER**!

REPLAY EDITOR

Your recent matches are recorded in the Replays feature. Reviewing battles helps you learn from your mistakes. Highlight the one you want to watch, hit play, and enjoy the show!

SPEED

In Replays, you can speed up or slow down your match recordings. For example, you can slow things down to relive an epic all-terrain kart jump or speed up a full-on build battle to create a time-lapse video.

CAMERA TYPE

There are lots of camera types to choose from! Drone Free gives you total control. If you're trying to set up a cool video of your performance, position the camera so that you create sweeping, action-packed views.

TOP LANDING TACTICS

Welcome aboard the Battle Bus—get ready for action and adventure! Below you lies an island packed with loot and teeming with foes. Plan your strategy as you leap into battle to give yourself the edge over your enemies.

BUS TRAIL

The Battle Bus flight path, or trail, is randomly generated, but it's always in a straight line. Many of your opponents will land near the trail and head towards the safe zone, located inside a white "safe circle". There is often **SERIOUS** fighting in built-up areas between the Bus trail and the safe circle. Use the trail to work out the location of these danger zones.

LANDING SPOT

Avoid landing in random places! When you're on the Battle Bus waiting to jump, open your map and place a pin on the area where you intend to touch down. This marker appears on-screen as a colored beam. You can use it to aim your skydive accurately and hit the right landing spot.

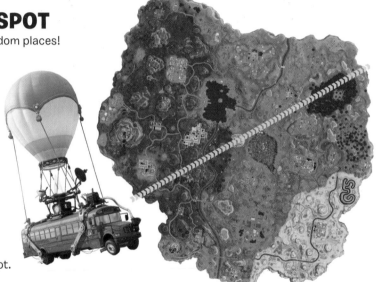

JUMPING AND LANDING

As the Battle Bus flies over the island at the start of the game, a jumping countdown begins. Once the time is up, you can press jump at any time. You'll skydive from the Bus, but you can open up your glider whenever you want. The glider auto-opens as you near the ground. Jumping first isn't always the best move, and neither is being the last to leave the Bus! Find a tactic that suits you.

SKYDIVING STRATEGY

Once you descend to 50 height units above the ground, your glider deploys automatically to slow your fall. It's best to avoid touching down on high ground. If you head for the ocean, you can get very low before the glider opens. As soon as you land, find a weapon as quickly as possible—it could save your life!

OBSERVATION

Take a look around as you drop through the air. Check out where the other 99 players are landing. Avoid spots where large numbers of newly-armed foes are already shooting it out. Also keep an eye out for loot—you may see piles of the stuff! Try to land near it and get ready for combat by loading up with weapons and supplies.

DID YOU KNOW?

If you land on top of a building, smash through the roof with your pickaxe. You'll collect building materials and, if there's an attic, you may find a treasure chest!

EXPLORE THE ISLAND

When you begin playing *Fortnite*, explore every part of the island. As you become a more seasoned player, focus on three or four areas, ideally located near to each other. Get to know them **INSIDE OUT**! You'll get a feel for where to find loot, the best highground sniping spots, chest-spawning locations, places to take cover in firefights, and more. Remember—knowledge is power!

LEAP INTO ACTION!

Here are some must-know landing tips and early-game survival advice:

- If you want to land sooner, skydiving is faster. Freefall as long as you can, then deploy your glider as you get close to the ground. For added speed, glide towards your landing zone at a diagonal angle.

- After you've armed yourself, survey your surroundings. Listen out for enemy activity, then start to harvest building materials with your pickaxe.

- Don't jump into a battle unless you feel confident you can win. *Fortnite* is all about survival, so when in doubt, run and hide—and live to fight another time!

23

MAP LOCATIONS REVEALED

When you're plummeting down onto the *Fortnite* island, you'll see **LOADS** of named locations on the map. Each area has its good points and its bad ones, but this handy guide will help you to pick the right drop zone to nail your landing strategy!

JUNK JUNCTION

Piled high with destroyed vehicles, Junk Junction definitely lives up to its name. There aren't many opportunities for rare loot here, but you can get your fill of metal and ammo before making your way inland.

HAUNTED HILLS

If you spook easily then make sure to steer your glider well away from this cemetery. If not, then don't be afraid to root around the crypts and mausoleum to find decent weapons and plentiful ammo.

PLEASANT PARK

Drop into this suburban neighborhood for some easy, if ordinary, swag. You won't find too many chests or vantage points, so empty the residences quickly and head to a more central locale.

SNOBBY SHORES

On the western coast of the map lies the gated community of Snobby Shores. The area is full of mid-level loot, including some decent weaponry, but it usually gets ensnared by the storm circle pretty quickly.

THE NORTH

JUNK JUNCTION

HAUNTED HILLS

PLEASANT PARK

LOOT LAKE

SNOBBY SHORES

LOOT LAKE

Enter the fray as you land, by diving headfirst into the central area of Loot Lake! The open water leaves no hiding place for campers, but what it lacks in cover, it more than makes up for in sweet, sweet swag.

RISKY REELS

This eerily abandoned drive-thru is perfect for metal scavengers thanks to the dozens of cars. It also seems to be full to the brim with swag, and the air rings with the buzz of many golden loot chests.

WAILING WOODS

Deep within a thicket of large trees, there's an outpost protected by a maze, where you can find ammo and weapons. The area is littered with shield mushrooms and camper vans that can be harvested for metal.

LAZY LINKS

Tired of the shooting and building routine? Then head over to Lazy Links for some golf! It may not have much loot, but it does have 18 holes for you to whack a ball around—hopefully you'll stay alive to finish a few!

TOMATO TEMPLE

What was once a simple restaurant franchise has now morphed into a place of fried-food worship. There's incredible loot in the temple's labyrinthine depths, though it can be quite difficult to find your way out!

LONELY LODGE

On the eastern map, you'll see a wooden lodge nestled in the middle of a forest campsite, making the area a great source of wood. There's a good amount of basic loot and mushrooms to boost your shield.

LAZY LINKS

RISKY REELS

TOMATO TEMPLE

WAILING WOODS

LONELY LODGE

©2018, Epic Games, Inc.

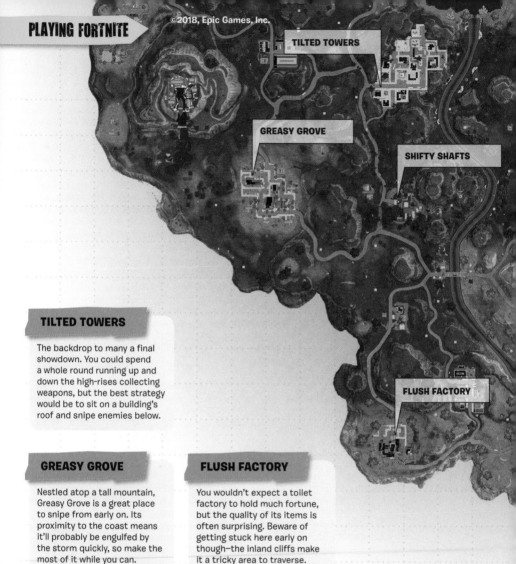

TILTED TOWERS

GREASY GROVE

SHIFTY SHAFTS

FLUSH FACTORY

TILTED TOWERS

The backdrop to many a final showdown. You could spend a whole round running up and down the high-rises collecting weapons, but the best strategy would be to sit on a building's roof and snipe enemies below.

GREASY GROVE

Nestled atop a tall mountain, Greasy Grove is a great place to snipe from early on. Its proximity to the coast means it'll probably be engulfed by the storm quickly, so make the most of it while you can.

FLUSH FACTORY

You wouldn't expect a toilet factory to hold much fortune, but the quality of its items is often surprising. Beware of getting stuck here early on though–the inland cliffs make it a tricky area to traverse.

SHIFTY SHAFTS

This industrial area has lots of valuable loot hidden away in the derelict mines. The open expanses are perfect for sniping enemies in neighboring areas: Tilted Towers and Greasy Grove.

DUSTY DIVOT

This former meteor crater has been swamped by flora and prefab modules stocked with weapons. Its central location often makes it a flashpoint for endgame standoffs, but it's worth a visit for the loot.

SALTY SPRINGS

Perfectly located at the center of the island, and with various treasure hotspots, Salty Springs may well be the best place to drop in, particularly if you want to search for loot at your own pace.

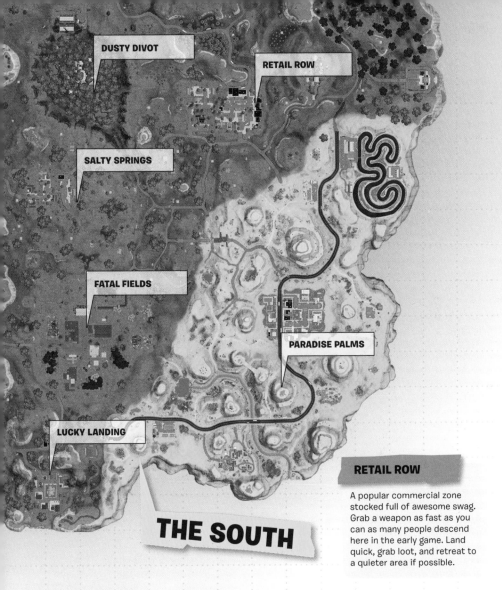

DUSTY DIVOT

RETAIL ROW

SALTY SPRINGS

FATAL FIELDS

PARADISE PALMS

LUCKY LANDING

THE SOUTH

RETAIL ROW

A popular commercial zone stocked full of awesome swag. Grab a weapon as fast as you can as many people descend here in the early game. Land quick, grab loot, and retreat to a quieter area if possible.

FATAL FIELDS

An agricultural haven to the south, Fatal Fields can be more unforgiving than it looks. The farmhouse and barns offer some loot, but the surrounding plains can leave you a sitting duck if exploring unprepared.

LUCKY LANDING

Some place names don't suit the location at all and this is one of them! Light on loot and dangerously far away from the center, you'd be better off skimming over the cherry blossoms to Paradise Palms.

PARADISE PALMS

The island's southeast corner recently transformed into a desert resort, complete with its own hotel! The hotel has the best of the loot, otherwise the area's pretty barren. Take a trip here for some unusual sights.

GAME SCREEN ESSENTIALS

Once you've landed, the Battle Royale begins ... so watch out! Enemies are everywhere, and they want to eliminate you **NOW**. To navigate and keep an eye on your friends and foes, you'll need to master the game screen.

TEAM HEALTH

In a squad or a duo, you need to look out for your teammates. These bars will help you to monitor their health. If one of the bars starts to go down and turns red, a teammate has been injured and may need reviving. When the bar vanishes, it's all over—they've been eliminated!

COMPASS

This navigation tool will help you find your way around the island. Each time you place a pin on the map, a colored icon appears on your compass. This acts as a marker to guide you toward your destination.

ELIMINATION FEED

This feed provides info on each elimination of your teammates and enemies during the game. It tells you who took them out and what weaponry was used.

knocked out   with a shotgun
eliminated   with a rifle
finally eliminated
eliminated   with an SMG
finally eliminated

DID YOU KNOW?

The game screen looks scarily busy at first and you'll need to put in some time to take it all in! Once you're familiar with it, and have learned techniques such as shifting quickly between Build and Combat modes, your game will **SERIOUSLY** improve.

HEALTH BARS

Your health and shield points are shown here. Players begin with 100 health and no shield. Both can be restored or boosted up to a maximum 100 points.

GAME CLOCK

At regular intervals, the game chooses an area of the map to be the safe circle. A blue clock counts down until the next storm. When it hits zero, the timer turns purple and a second countdown begins. The storm is now advancing and the clock shows you how long it'll take to reach the safe circle's outer edge.

MINI-MAP

On the mini-map, your position is marked by a white arrow that points in the direction you're facing; on-screen labeling tells you the area you are in. It shows your distance from both the safe circle and the lethal purple storm. If you are outside the safe circle, a straight line shows you the quickest, most direct route to reach it and move inside it. Your squad members are displayed as small arrows.

PLAYER COUNT

This displays the remaining number of players, ticking them off as they're taken out! At the beginning of the game it falls fast, as less experienced players land and are swiftly eliminated by seasoned *Fortnite* gamers.

INVENTORY

Click on this to display an inventory of the collected loot, traps, and materials contained in your backpack. Arrange your weapons and items into a quick-access order that suits your gameplay. You can also "Split" or "Drop" materials. "Split" means you'll drop half of your selected material, while "Drop" allows you to drop as much as you like.

WOOD, BRICK, METAL

A running total of the different building materials you harvest with your pickaxe is displayed here. Each single structure you construct will cost ten units of whatever material you build with.

BUILD MENU

Enter Build Mode to allow you to cycle through available walls, ramps, floors and roofs. On PC or Mac, these can be attributed to selected buttons. On consoles, scroll through or set to Builder Pro in the Settings menu.

ITEMS HOTBAR

There are six slots to store items. Your pickaxe defaults to the first slot. On PC or Mac, each slot can be assigned to individual buttons. On consoles, toggle between the pickaxe and items, then scroll to the item you want.

29

LOOTING: THE BASICS

In order to progress in *Fortnite,* you need to load yourself up with loot. The more you find, the more equipped you'll be to fend off foes when that storm closes in. First up: materials. Without these, you won't be able to build.

START HARVESTING

From the moment you land, look for ways to "harvest" so you can instantly start to build if required. Almost every object on the map is harvestable, so you'll never run out of options. The three materials you need are wood, brick, and metal.

WOOD
The original and best! In theory wood is weakest, but it's quickest to harvest and build. Crucially, it has more health than brick and metal when initially placed. You can also see through its cracks.
Source from: trees, pallets, roofs, walls–anything made from wood!
At full-build: 200 health points.

BRICK
Stronger than wood, but slower to spawn. A superior maximum health is beneficial in the long run, so use when you're not under immediate attack, where one shot can see it collapse.
Source from: rocks, walls, roofs, floors–anything made from brick!
At full-build: 300 health points.

METAL
Harder to destroy providing it's at max health. While metal is the strongest, it's initially weak and takes the longest to fully spawn. Best reserved for a tactical endgame showdown.
Source from: vehicles, fencing, crates, walls–anything metal!
At full-build: 400 health points.

YOUR PICKAXE IS YOUR PAL!
Everyone lands on the map with nothing but a glider and a pickaxe, both of which remain with you by default to the end. Use your pickaxe purely to harvest and hack away at objects quickly and smartly. Don't rely on your pickaxe in battle; you'll need to be super-close to an enemy and won't stand a chance once they start shooting.

HIT THE MARK

The moment you wave your pickaxe at an object, a purple circle appears. This is a moving target to show exactly where you need to strike. Pro tip: press yourself right up against the object so the marker barely moves, resulting in a quicker and more effective harvest.

THINK BEFORE YOU HARVEST

It's tempting to roam the map destroying every object you come across. However, that can eat up vital seconds and warn others of your presence. Smashing down a wall or roof of a building makes you an easy target if someone's nearby. Smaller items like beds and desks offer little reward, so don't waste time ransacking rooms when you don't need to. Be disciplined!

HARVEST AS YOU RUN

Remember, you **ALWAYS** need materials. Taking cover behind rocks and trees in the endgame will only last so long before you need to build. As you run with the storm, quickly swing at nearby objects to boost your supply for when it matters most. Brick and metal will serve you best when you reach the final five.

DID YOU KNOW?

Vehicles make **A LOT** of noise. If you need a quick metal fix when in company, try to avoid harvesting from cars and trucks. They produce the most, but raise an alarm.

HARVESTING ESSENTIALS

Knowing how much you need of each material, and which items provide the highest resource, will help prioritize when and how you harvest. Our suggestions are as follows:

• **PALLETS** offer approx 40-60 **WOOD** per harvest.

• **ROCKS** offer approx 30-60 **BRICK** per harvest.

• **VEHICLES** offer approx 20-30 **METAL** per harvest.

Aim for 100 materials for early-game combat, 300 materials for mid-game combat, and simply as much as you can possibly gather for the endgame.

LOOTING: WHAT TO FIND

Materials help you build, take cover, and gain battle-winning vantage points. Items, from weapons to traps and healing consumables, maintain your survival. Utilize the map–loot can be located **EVERYWHERE!**

WHERE AND HOW TO LOOT

There's no definitive guide to exactly where items will be situated in *Fortnite*, but early on it's best to hit high ground or secluded areas. If you're in a busy town, others may beat you to it, leaving you open to attack with zero resources. Some loot spawns on its own, while other loot come in useful packs via chests, boxes, supply drops, and, er, purple llamas!

GOLDEN LOOT CHESTS

You'll either hear an angelic hum that increases as you get closer to it or spot a golden glow. If the chest is high, loot might drop to lower ground as it spills out.

AMMO BOXES

Weapons are useless without bullets, so don't pass an ammo box without opening it up. Keep an eye out, as they're less obvious than the golden loot chests.

SUPPLY DROPS

Listen for a plane and look for a blue flare to mark its landing. These contain more advanced items, so bear in mind others will be paying close attention.

IN-GAME ENEMIES

Often the best way to acquire loot is in an elimination. A player's entire inventory scatters at the scene allowing you to hoover up key items without relying on random searches. Double win!

HEALING AND SHIELDING

Like weapons, healing items range from Common to Legendary, so some are easier to come by than others. Note: shields are crucial for winning battles!

BANDAGE

Restores 15 health. Up to 15 bandages per slot. They need four seconds to use and must be applied standing still. You can only restore up to 75 health.

MEDKIT

Restores full health in one go. Up to three medkits per slot. They need ten seconds to use, while standing still, which can make you vulnerable to attacks by your foes.

APPLE

Restores 5 health. Must be consumed immediately and takes one second to use. Unlike other items, they are only found on the ground near apple trees.

SMALL SHIELD POTION
Adds 25 shield points. You can stack up to ten small shield potions in a single slot. Each potion takes two seconds to use, but can only take you up to 50 shield.

SHIELD POTION

Adds 50 shield. Up to two shield potions in a single slot. It takes five seconds to use. You can use two potions—one after the other—to take you up to 100 shield.

SLURP JUICE

Adds 25 shield/health, granting points to both every second for 37.5 seconds. Up to two slurps per slot. It takes two seconds to use; can take you up to 75 shield/health.

CHUG JUG

Adds full health and full shield in one go. It takes 15 seconds to use. This super-healing drink doesn't stack, so you can only carry one at a time in a single slot.

SHIELD MUSHROOM

Adds 5 shield. Mushrooms must be consumed immediately and they take one second to use. They are found around shady wooded or swampy areas.

LOOTING TIPS

Looting and healing can be complicated! Here's what you should know when loading your backpack:

- Steering clear of a supply drop can work in your favor. Everyone will be after its contents, giving you the chance to snipe those who run towards it.

- What you've got doesn't have to be your lot. If you spot better loot but your backpack is full, switch out unwanted items for new ones.

- Health is the green bar, shield is the blue bar. Shields act as a forcefield around your health, so top up to max shield at every opportunity.

- Consuming items takes time. Consider your surroundings as you'll be a sitting duck. Building a small fort is a good way to take a healing break.

TRAPS (AND THE PORT-A-FORT)

Lay these bad boys down for serious combat—and serious fun!

DAMAGE TRAP

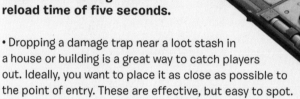

Place these on walls, floors, and roofs and wait for an enemy to trigger the spikes. Each trap inflicts 150 damage with a reload time of five seconds.

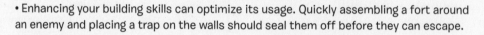

• Dropping a damage trap near a loot stash in a house or building is a great way to catch players out. Ideally, you want to place it as close as possible to the point of entry. These are effective, but easy to spot.

• Enhancing your building skills can optimize its usage. Quickly assembling a fort around an enemy and placing a trap on the walls should seal them off before they can escape.

• If all else fails when in a tight spot, simply drop one of these to frighten your foe. Chances are they'll step back, giving you a quick second to figure out your next move.

LAUNCH PAD

BOING! Create a base using materials and then place a pad on top. You'll spring yourself into the air and coast with your glider. Ideal for quickly reaching high ground when under attack.

• Once you've placed a pad, you can't pick it back up. Therefore, it's free for other players to use should they come across it.

• These are great for escaping enemies and evading the storm. You move quicker and further when airborne.

• Watch out! Flying through the air using a glider makes you easy to spot. Decent shooters could land fatal blows, while others will be able to determine your location.

PORT-A-FORT

This epic, funnel-like structure sprouts from a small metallic ball you hold in your inventory (not the trap slot, like the others). Made from metal, it provides an instant fort without needing to construct one–and it's **MASSIVE!**

• Unless you're using it as a decoy, drop the fort as close to you as possible. That way you can enter it quickly without running across ground.

• Bouncy tires at the base propel you to the top and protect you from fall damage. A blueprint of where the fort will spawn appears prior to you releasing it.

• These aren't just for protection–you can throw them like a grenade or bomb. Use them to obliterate structures or to trap enemies inside. You can even stack them!

COZY CAMPFIRE

If you can't stand the heat, go get some heat! This heals at a rate of 2 health points per second and lasts for 25 seconds. Great when playing Squads as it can heal all players at the same time.

BOUNCER TRAP

Spring forward, upward, and sideways! These bouncers inflict zero fall damage, so they're perfect for dropping from high ground without losing health. Alternatively, use them to escape foes or as a super-speedy way to rush an enemy's base.

WEAPONS: THE BASICS

The weapons used in *Fortnite* are so numerous and varied that it will take you a while to get used to them all, especially due to the random spawns. Heed the advice shown here to become an all-knowing weapons **EXPERT!**

WEAPON RARITIES

There are five tiers of weapon rarity (see below)—the higher the rarity, the stronger the weapon's stats. Not every weapon in the game is available in every rarity, so don't search for a Legendary tactical shotgun—it doesn't exist. The general rule is the better the rarity, the better the stats—but not every single stat will increase if the rarity is higher.

COMMON	UNCOMMON	RARE	EPIC	LEGENDARY

CHOOSING YOUR WEAPONS

It might be tempting to grab every Epic and Legendary you see, but it shouldn't be the only factor to determine your loadout. Aim for a variety of weapons, disregarding rarity, and consider the situation around you. For instance, if the storm circle is at its smallest, you won't need to shoot very far, so you should favor assault rifles, pistols, and shotguns in this scenario.

CONSIDER YOUR SURROUNDINGS

The vantage points and pitfalls of areas should also inform your loadout. Sniper rifles are lethal over the open plains of Fatal Fields. LMGs and assault rifles are perfect for duck-and-cover encounters in built up areas like Retail Row, while SMGs and shotguns are best for claustrophobic encounters in the houses of Snobby Shores.

CHANGING GUNS

Quickly switching weapons can create clever combos and delay some less desired weapon attributes, such as lengthy reloads. For instance, you can unload a whole SMG clip into an enemy to deplete most of their health, then swap to a shotgun to finish them off and avoid reloading the SMG.

DON'T (HOLD) SHOOT!

Learning how to control weapons is a skill that will take a long time to develop, but you can help yourself by not making a basic error–don't keep the shoot button held down! The longer you hold the button, the wilder the spray (or "bloom") will become, making it harder to control the gun and reducing your accuracy.

ANY GUN IS BETTER THAN NONE

Some players will steer clear of certain weapons that don't meet their high standards. Don't be that person! You can always replace a gun you don't like when you find a different one, but it's better to have a gun and not need one than to need a gun and not have one.

FINALLY: DON'T LISTEN TO US ...

... or anyone else, for that matter. The best way to play *Fortnite* is the way **YOU'RE** most comfortable with. Many people will tell you how the game should be played, but if you're finding success and having fun picking off opponents with a pistol from a mile away then keep it up!

WEAPONS: STATS & RARITIES

Use this guide to rate your weaponry. The higher the stat scale, the better the weapon. Each card's background color signifies the weapon's lowest rarity tier availability (see page 36). Colored boxes indicate other rarity tier availability.

PISTOLS

Often underestimated, the humble pistol isn't the showiest of weapons, nor does it pack the most punch. However, it's indispensible in short-range gunfights as long as you have a steady aim or a static target.

REVOLVER

The revolver packs a hefty punch but has an achingly slow fire rate and a small magazine. It's best to use it at a point-blank range when you have an enemy cornered in a small area.

| DAMAGE |
| FIRE RATE |
| MAG SIZE |
| RELOAD |

RARITIES:

PISTOL

A standard-issue pistol excels at a short range. The rapid fire rate makes it one of the handiest choices for close-range combat. Just don't try to pick anyone off from long-distance!

| DAMAGE |
| FIRE RATE |
| MAG SIZE |
| RELOAD |

RARITIES:

SUPPRESSED

This upgraded version of the regular pistol has the added bonus of being almost completely silent. A great weapon to have in your hand if you're stealthily sneaking into enemy territory.

| DAMAGE |
| FIRE RATE |
| MAG SIZE |
| RELOAD |

RARITIES:

HAND CANNON

The most powerful of all the pistols is also the slowest. However, the sacrifice in speed is well worth it as it can take down an enemy with just a couple of shots. Make sure to keep it loaded.

| DAMAGE |
| FIRE RATE |
| MAG SIZE |
| RELOAD |

RARITIES:

SUB-MACHINE GUNS

Blessed with rapid fire and a huge magazine, but cursed with a wide spray, the SMG can be great for beginners shooting from the hip, and deadly in the hands of a pro.

SMG

Fairly weak but very fast, the SMG is great for noobs getting used to aiming. Its long reload can leave you stranded, but you can combine it with a shotgun to cover its shortcomings.

| DAMAGE |
| FIRE RATE |
| MAG SIZE |
| RELOAD |

RARITIES:

SUPPRESSED

Trading in some of its speed for increased damage, faster reloads and a muted muzzle, the suppressed SMG is a good progression gun for anyone acquainted with the SMG's erratic spray.

| DAMAGE |
| FIRE RATE |
| MAG SIZE |
| RELOAD |

RARITIES:

LIGHT MACHINE GUNS

Sometimes bigger is better, and light machine guns are proof of that. Their rapid fire rate and huge magazine make them great for clearing crowds.

MINIGUN

DAMAGE	■□□□□
FIRE RATE	■■■■■
MAG SIZE	N/A
RELOAD	N/A

Who needs reloads? A minigun has all the ammo it needs in one clip. Often hard to handle, its destructive potential is immense.

RARITIES: ■

LMG

DAMAGE	■■□□□
FIRE RATE	■■■□□
MAG SIZE	■■■■□
RELOAD	■■□□□

LMGs are great at tearing through swathes of enemies, but have a fairly long reload time, so plan reloads wisely.

RARITIES: ■

ASSAULT RIFLES

A happy medium between fire rate and damage, assault rifles are particularly effective for causing a lot of damage at short to medium distances. They suffer over longer ranges, however.

M16

DAMAGE	■■□□□
FIRE RATE	■■■□□
MAG SIZE	■■■■□
RELOAD	■■■■□

Entry-level assault weapon with great damage, decent fire rate, and a large magazine.

RARITIES: ■ ■

SCAR

DAMAGE	■■□□□
FIRE RATE	■■■■□
MAG SIZE	■■■■□
RELOAD	■■■■■

Like the M16, the SCAR is a good all-round weapon, but with better damage and quicker reloads.

RARITIES: ■

BURST

DAMAGE	■■□□□
FIRE RATE	■■■□□
MAG SIZE	■■■□□
RELOAD	■■■■□

Short, controlled sprays of bullets make this weapon more suited to veterans with a steady aim.

RARITIES: ■ ■

SCOPED

DAMAGE	■■□□□
FIRE RATE	■■□□□
MAG SIZE	■■■■□
RELOAD	■■■■□

The sighted scope atop this gun assists aiming, but forfeits some of the damage and fire rate.

RARITIES: ■

BURST (FAMAS)

Another for those with a steady hand, the FAMAS has increased damage but an average reload time. The prominent sight makes up for the significant recoil, which can affect your aim.

DAMAGE	■■■□□
FIRE RATE	■■■□□
MAG SIZE	■■■□□
RELOAD	■■■□□

RARITIES: ■

THERMAL SCOPED

A dream for scouts and infiltrators, this assault weapon has a thermal scope attached, which highlights any potential targets. It also happens to be the most powerful assault weapon.

DAMAGE	■■■□□
FIRE RATE	■■■□□
MAG SIZE	■■□□□
RELOAD	■■■□□

RARITIES: ■

SHOTGUNS

The best weapon for close-range combat without exception. Shotguns have immense power and a usually average fire rate, but you may need to duck and hide if the small amount of ammo runs out and you need to do a lengthy reload.

TACTICAL

Out of all shotguns, this one lends itself to rapid fire, making it a deadly close-range option. Unfortunately, it has a sluggish reload that could be the difference between life and death!

DAMAGE
FIRE RATE
MAG SIZE
RELOAD   **RARITIES:**

PUMP

The slowest of the shotguns, the pump-action actually causes the most damage per hit. Its quicker reload is balanced by a small magazine, but it's still a viable and deadly gun.

DAMAGE
FIRE RATE
MAG SIZE
RELOAD   **RARITIES:**

HEAVY

The rarest shotgun is probably the most balanced of the bunch. It's a rarity to find, but should immediately demand a place among your weapon slots if you do come across one.

DAMAGE
FIRE RATE
MAG SIZE
RELOAD   **RARITIES:**

SNIPER RIFLES

If you'd prefer to stay far away from skirmishes, then the sniper rifle is for you. They have tremendous power over a long distance, but require you to have an awesome aim to make the shot in the first place.

SEMI-AUTO

The only sniper rifle that doesn't need reloading after every shot. This quick-fire action makes up for the reduced damage and is probably the best entry-level sniper rifle for noobs.

DAMAGE
FIRE RATE
MAG SIZE
RELOAD   **RARITIES:**

BOLT-ACTION

Bested only by the rocket launcher in terms of power per shot, the bolt-action sniper is lethal for those with the ability to wield it. The scope makes picking off distant targets a breeze.

DAMAGE
FIRE RATE
MAG SIZE
RELOAD   **RARITIES:**

HUNTING RIFLE

Lacking the scope of its counterparts, the hunting rifle is possibly the trickiest gun to master. However, its decent fire rate and quick reload raise it above the other snipers.

DAMAGE
FIRE RATE
MAG SIZE
RELOAD   **RARITIES:**

GRENADES

Guns are all well and good, but if your aim isn't that great, or you're faced with a crowd of enemies, then grenades are your new best friend. The effects of grenades vary greatly, but they can always help you out of tight situations.

GRENADE

DAMAGE ▣▣▣□□

The bog-standard lobbed grenade can cause damage over a wide radius.

CLINGER

DAMAGE ▣▣▣▣□

The clinger is a sticky mess that will adhere to players or vehicles wherever they go.

IMPULSE GRENADE

DAMAGE N/A

This doesn't cause any damage, but propels anyone within range up and away.

STINK BOMB

DAMAGE ▣□□□□

A smelly throwable that will cause toxic damage to recipients over a period of time.

BOOGIE BOMB

DAMAGE N/A

Sometimes you just need a distraction to get you out of a sticky situation! Throw the boogie bomb to start an impromptu disco, rendering enemies useless at anything except throwing shapes.

LAUNCHERS

If you can't be bothered to toss a grenade yourself then a) you're lazy, and b) you don't have to—launchers can do the work for you! Each launcher propels a different explosive much farther than you could ever fling it anyway.

ROCKET LAUNCHER

A weapon that will send enemies scattering in fear, the rocket launcher causes explosive damage to a wide area. Ammo is rare for this weapon so be sure to make each rocket count!

DAMAGE ▣▣▣▣□
FIRE RATE ▣▣□□□
MAG SIZE ▣□□□□
RELOAD ▣▣▣□□

RARITIES: ▣▣

GRENADE LAUNCHER

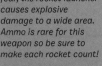

Possessing the ability to lob grenades in an arc, this firearm is somewhat hit and miss. It can cause a great deal of damage, but it more often relies on luck than any amount of skill.

DAMAGE ▣▣▣▣▣
FIRE RATE ▣▣□□□
MAG SIZE ▣▣□□□
RELOAD ▣▣□□□

RARITIES: ▣▣

BUILDING: THE BASICS

Building may seem complicated and unnecessary if you're new to *Fortnite*. It's easier to just grab some weapons and look for the fight, right? Wrong. You'll never master the game and attain a Victory Royale without building.

HOW DO YOU ACTUALLY BUILD?

To create a structure, you'll need to have looted enough wood, metal, or brick. Once you've got a decent stockpile, switch to the Build menu during a game. After selecting which building piece you want, it will appear as a blueprint in front of you. Click "build" to confirm your selection and in a few short seconds it will be complete.

WALLS

Any structure takes time to reach full strength. The transparent blue sections will quickly take on the form of your chosen material. Wood is the quickest material to build with, but brick and metal are stronger and can take more damage!

The first thing you should try building is a wall. These might seem simple and ineffective but build four well-placed walls and you've got your first base!

Walls are also one of the most effective defenses in the game. Even if you've got full health and maximum shield, throwing down a wall is the best form of defense. Not only will it absorb the damage, it will make it harder for your enemy to see where you are—or what you're planning!

Walls may be the best form of defense, but throw a quick ramp into the mix and you can turn defense into attack! The best way to gain an instant advantage over your opponent is to get higher than them, so build three walls and a ramp and you can take cover and quickly pop up to take your shot!

However, before you worry too much about combat, you can use ramps for easier tasks. Use them to access loot that's high up or to quickly climb a mountain. Or, if you're up for the action, to climb into an enemy base!

RAMPS

This classic combat technique is easy to master and achievable in seconds. Three walls, one ramp, and you've gained an advantage on the battlefield.

FLOORS

Of the four main building shapes, floors are the only ones that don't offer an immediate advantage to your attack or defense. Yet many players use these to finish off the top of their base. Unlike using a ramp or a roof, floors allow you to maintain an easy view around your entire base. However, they will also leave you exposed to enemy fire.

As you develop your base-building skills, floors can be used to create more intricate walkways.

But if you're just starting out, floors are at their simple best if you need to hurry across water or between mountains. Simply lay them down ahead of you as you run across!

PRO TIP
If you're new to building in *Fortnite*, then practice as much as you can. Choose a quiet, secluded location where you can start experimenting by building simple bases and structures.

A floor on top of a short base will leave you open to attack from every angle.

ROOFS

You'll probably find you use roofs less than the other elements, but when you do use them, they can be one of the most important parts of any structure!

Because of the unique shape of the roof pieces, you can be really creative when using them. For example, if you've built a tower, try placing them around the top to act as makeshift turrets – their pyramid shape will make it so much harder for opponents to identify where you are!

With no roof on your structure you can peer down on enemies, but anyone higher than your position will have an advantage over you!

DID YOU KNOW?

You'll need to master building to stand any chance of Victory Royale, but be smart about when you build. A simple ramp to reach some loot could go unnoticed, but building a tall base in the early stages will alert other players to your location and may soon be lost to the storm anyway!

BUILDING: HOW TO EDIT

By now you will have tried building simple shapes, so it's time to learn how you can develop your structures. Not only will they start to look much cooler, but they'll become even more valuable to your gameplay.

EDITING STRUCTURES

You can edit any wall, ramp, floor, or roof with the click of a button. Simply point your cursor at the shape and you can quickly enter the Edit menu. Each one is made up of either a 2 x 2 or a 3 x 3 grid, and by editing the squares of the grid you can drastically change the way your builds work.

Once you get the hang of it, you can pre-edit your structures before you even build them!

DID YOU KNOW?

You can't edit structures built by an enemy, but you can destroy them. Swing away with your axe to undo all their hard work! You don't gain much of the material they used, though, so don't waste too much time doing this.

ROOFS

HUNTER'S PERCH

We've seen how a roofless base can leave you open to aerial attack. This perch offers you the protection of a roof but still gives you an attacking advantage over anyone below.

Build a tower with a roof at the top, then edit a corner of the roof to create a quarter pyramid. This leaves you with defensive coverage on three sides but gives you an opening to spot any approaching enemies.

If your roof is high enough, you may not lose any defensive cover at all. If you open fire on an enemy but fail to finish them off, simply retreat back into the cavern of your roof—your enemies will struggle to find the right angle to return fire.

DID YOU KNOW?

As the safe zone gets smaller, you may find elements of your base are facing the wrong way. Don't panic! A quick edit can rotate anything so it faces the action again.

FLOORS

CORNER BALCONY

The corner floor is impressive while still being easy to build. Select one corner of your 2 x 2 floor grid and confirm the move.

This simple build resembles a curved balcony, giving you a great view of the area around you and, if you need it, some solid protection if you crouch behind the balcony wall.

But remember: anyone could approach from behind so be sure to check behind you, too!

HALF FLOOR

By editing two adjacent squares of a 2 x 2 floor grid, you can create a half floor.

It might not sound like much, but this edit creates a valuable barrier all along one side of your floor panels. This'll make it harder for your enemies to inflict damage if you're crossing water or running towards some valuable loot.

However, it does reduce the width of your flooring, making it easier to fall off, so proceed with caution!

FULL FLOOR

It's always good fun to edit your floor builds. Doing so can have some benefits, but it isn't always worth it. One of the best uses for floors is to get from one high location to another without having to climb down. Just lay floors out into thin air!

WALLS

DOOR WALL

By editing the two lower-central squares of a wall's 3 x 3 grid, you can add a doorway. This is particularly useful at the foundation of a taller base, like a sniper tower. It's common to fall out during combat, so having a door lets you get straight back inside again with no delay.

WINDOW WALL

We've looked at how walls are the quickest and easiest form of defense, but there's more to them than meets the eye. Adding a window to a wall won't reduce how much cover it offers you, but it will give you the ability to return fire!

2/3 WALL

Select the top three squares of your wall's grid and confirm the changes to create a 2/3 wall. If you're taking fire, crouch behind it and move position before jumping back up and returning fire. Your opponents won't know where you'll reappear, so will lose time adjusting their aim.

RAMPS

ROTATION

There's one common problem when building a ramp in an enclosed space ... if you don't jump up, you can get trapped underneath it. A simple edit to change its direction will give you another chance to get on the top side! In the Edit menu, click and drag one of the arrows and your ramp will rotate in your chosen direction.

CORNER STAIRS

One of our favorite edits is so simple, but has outstanding results. In the Edit menu of your ramp, highlight an L shape and select "confirm". It will transform into a narrow ramp that climbs upward at a right-angle. It will help disorientate your enemies, and the newly-created bannister looks good and offers extra protection from incoming fire.

U-BEND STAIRS

Even more handy are the stairs you can create by highlighting a U shape. These ramps have sharp-alternating turns in a small amount of space.

PRO TIP

If you're building a tower base, edit the shapes below you as you progress upwards. This will block the path of enemies and make you harder to reach.

BUILDING: ADVANCED TIPS

Now you've practiced the basics of walls, floors, ramps, and roofs, it's time to develop your abilities. Most matches of *Fortnite* are won and lost by the players' building skills, so developing these is key to your success!

RAMP AND WALL

Welcome to one of the most simple builds in the game. Simple, but highly effective when out in the open. Start by building a quick wall then install a ramp behind it. Whether your enemy aims for you or your build, they'll struggle to deliver enough damage. Meanwhile, you can quickly pop up to open fire then duck down again to reload behind cover. Winning!

The stronger the materials you build with, the longer they'll last in battle.

SOLID FOUNDATIONS

Just as in real life, anything you build in *Fortnite* must be connected to solid ground. You can build a huge tower, but if it's only grounded by one room then the whole thing can be destroyed with minimal effort—sending you crashing down. Try to "connect" your builds to the ground in as many places as possible and they'll be much stronger during battle.

Shoot the bottom of a large ramp and the rest will collapse, too.

BASE PROTECTORS

As the size of the safe zone shrinks, you'll find more players building tall towers to try to evade enemy fire. You should definitely do the same. When you've reached a safe height, surround the top of your base with ledges made of floors or ramps. These will make it extra difficult for anyone to build next to you and try to infiltrate your base!

GIANT TEAM TENT

A simple trick is to place a roof over an injured teammate so they can heal under cover. Here we take that technique to the next level! Pre-edit a roof by selecting one corner of its 2 x 2 grid and laying it down. Repeat this three times and you'll be left with a giant team tent. Perfect for using a campfire to recharge your squad's health.

These ledges keep you covered, but are easily shot at and destroyed. Don't stand on the same one too long!

Building your team tent on a slight hill means you can run in and out of its protection quickly to check for danger.

IT'S A TRAP!

If you're hiding somewhere secret, lay down floors and walls to tempt players to your position. This sounds like an odd tactic, but listen up: set a trap on one of the walls and it'll catch intruders by surprise, damaging their health and sending them cowering away!

If a player activates your trap, the sound will also alert you to their position.

RAMP TO RIFT

Landing at locations on the edges of the map has huge looting benefits, but it also greatly increases the odds of the storm reaching you sooner. It's common to see players lose track of time and get swallowed by the storm! If you find yourself in this situation then start sprinting to safety, but don't panic. Look around you as you run-if you see a rift in the sky, run towards it and lay down ramps to get close. As soon as you hit the rift you'll blast high up into the sky, and you'll easily outrun the storm, gliding through the air!

RAMP RUSHING

Tall enemy bases can be full of traps, so your best way in is via ramps to the top (this will also be your easiest route back down). If your foe sees you coming they will open fire on you or your ramp, which could lead to a fatal drop back down to earth! By quickly building two ramps alongside each other, you will greatly improve your chances of safe passage to the top-your enemy won't be able to fire quickly enough to destroy them both!

MASTERING A TOWER BASE!

If you want to get better at building useful bases then this is the place to start. Practice this simple tower base and you'll master the skills and develop the ideas needed to go on and create your own designs. Many of the best bases we've seen while playing *Fortnite* have used these basic building principles as their starting point.

1 Build four walls to create a square room, making sure you remain in the middle of them all.

2 Standing with your back to one wall, select the ramp shape. As soon as you click "confirm," jump up to stay on top of it.

3 Walk to the top of your ramp and build four more walls, then another ramp in the opposite direction to your first ramp. Keep going until you reach your desired height, then finish it off with a level floor.

4 Build four more walls and a roof to finish the top of your structure. Add some windows and you'll have a perfect view of the surrounding area. Job done!

MOVEMENT FUNDAMENTALS

Right, it's time to get moving ... literally! Whether you're lurking on the edge of the circle or running amok through Retail Row, movement is a key strategy in *Fortnite*–and it starts from the second you leave the Bus. Make it count!

FROM A TO B

SHORT AND SHARP

Faster moving players are easier to spot, so keep sprints to quick bursts and scan the area for landmarks you can hide behind en route. Pick a direction and commit.

GO GRADUAL

Your aim is to stay within the safe zone, but there's no need to bust a gut to get there. Keep moving, but take your time to avoid areas that may leave you exposed.

BAG A BUSH

Tread terrain in crazy camouflage. Foes won't have time to gamble on every bush being a potential threat, so you'll avoid early hits and enjoy some added comedy!

SCOUT IN THE SHADE

Snazzy outfits are cool, but they stick out like a sore thumb against paths, roads and grass. Move in shadowy areas and buildings with lots of colors to stay hidden.

TROLLEY DASH

So much fun! Ideally used in Duos (the passenger shoots and builds while the teammate pushes), these can move at decent speeds, especially down hills!

ATK OK

Awesome all-terrain karts (ATK) allow an entire squad to drift around the map. But be warned–they make a lot of noise and enemies will know you're coming.

IN ENEMY TERRITORY

LOCATION LURKING

Approach areas from the edges. Players, especially noobs, are attracted to built-up towns due to the loot on offer, so circle cities and observe the situation. Don't compromise your position too early. Let others do the hard work before moving in.

CREEP, CRAWL AND CROUCH

Once you've gone high, be sure to go low! Footsteps are a key indicator of where foes are, but crouching is quieter and helps you find position without others noticing. You'll also benefit from steadier weapon accuracy, especially from a distance.

CHECK YOURSELF

Before entering battle, ensure you check **ALL** your surroundings. It's easy to stroll into spaces when spotting loot, but bear in mind someone could be waiting inside for you. Pitch up **OUTSIDE**, use your viewpoint, and get the drop on that unsuspecting enemy.

STAYING ALIVE

Oh no, you've been spotted! Avoid being shot with these top four tips:

• **KEEP MOVING!** Run, jump, and zigzag when out in the open. A moving target is harder to hit.

• **POINT AND PEEK!** When crouching under cover, line up your target and **THEN** peek out to get your shot away.

• **LOOK AROUND!** If running, look left, right, up, and down. You might find a safer spot to reassess your attack.

• **PLAY DUMB!** Pretend you haven't seen an enemy. They'll think you're an easy target when instead you're fully prepared.

COMBAT STRATEGIES

In *Fortnite*, you have to survive longer than the 99 other players. To win the game, you're going to need to fight. Use everything you've learned so far—movement, weapons, and building. Here are our essential combat strategies.

INVENTORY INTELLIGENCE

The random nature of looting means your success can vary wildly from game to game. Whatever weapons you find, build your plan around them! For example, if you've only got a shotgun, don't go firing through open fields, but take cover inside and go for close combat.

SNIPE AND MOVE

Not only is sniping one of the hardest skills, but it can also put you at risk. It's tempting to crouch and stare down your scope, but never remain still for too long. If you do, you may get sniped yourself! Move from a crouch to standing to a crouch, and so on. Moving sideways will also help.

PLAY MIND GAMES

You've spotted an enemy, fired off some rounds, but failed to finish them off. Now they know where you are—and they'll be angry! Using a quick build or the landscape, stay hidden but change position and come at them from another angle, catching them by surprise again!

THREE IS A CROWD

You will occasionally come across other players battling it out, either close-by or in the distance. Wait for one of them to triumph before making your move. It's likely they'll have lost health and won't be expecting you to charge in and finish off the job their recent victim started!

HIGH GROUND

Having a height advantage over an opponent can be the difference between success and failure, and this is particularly true as the safe zone shrinks throughout the match. Be it atop buildings or at the summit of your own structure: stay there. Let your opponents focus on building ramps—you can focus on eliminating them!

QUIET DESTINATION

When deciding where to land at the start of a game, consider the quieter areas on the outskirts of the Battle Royale map. There's a good chance you'll be alone to loot and will build up quite the arsenal. By the time the storm pushes you further into the action, other players may be low on ammo. Not you, though. You'll be armed to the teeth with some of the best weapons in the game!

COMBAT TIPS

- *If you're struggling to hold your aim on an opponent, try crouching as you line them up in your sights. It definitely improves accuracy!*

- *Whatever your style of combat, jumping up and down as you fight will make it so much harder for your enemies to critically damage you.*

- *Always keep extra shield potions or bandages in your inventory. They're often more valuable than different weapon variations.*

- *If you've taken damage in a fire fight and need to recharge your health or shield, always find some cover before doing so.*

- *Location is king. Before you give away your position, think what you'll gain from doing so. Will one elimination be worth it, or are you better off staying in the shadows?*

- *Don't waste grenades or rocket launcher ammo early on. As the battle rages on, there'll be more bases and more chances to have some fun with such weapons!*

- *Struggling to pick off an enemy perched on top of their tall base? Look at the bottom of it. If it's narrow enough, aim your fire there. Destroy that and they'll come tumbling down with it!*

- *Add window walls to every floor of your own base. Even if you can't access every window, your enemies won't know that. Whichever window you emerge firing from could catch them by surprise.*

1v1 COMBAT SCENARIOS

With 100 players taking part in every game, it's almost impossible to predict which way each one will go. But there are some scenarios that you can be prepared for.

WHEN YOU'RE IN CLOSE QUARTERS COMBAT

If you're inside a building and realize you have company then stand still around one side of a corner. Move to the right and you can peer around a corner without giving away your position. When you see someone coming, get ready to pounce—they won't be as ready as you are!

WHEN YOU RUN INTO AN ENEMY IN THE OPEN

It's common to run into other players when you're out in the open, especially when you're fleeing the storm. Novice players will hide behind trees or try to run away, but the best way to get out of this alive is to use the wall and ramp combo!

WHEN YOU'VE GOT A LOADED SNIPER RIFLE

Use your sniper rifle if you have the high ground and nobody knows your position. The opposition will be severely hurt if you land your shot, regardless of distance. If you blunder, don't reload. Change to your assault rifle or rapid-fire weapon to finish them off.

WHEN ATTACKING A BASE

In this situation it's easy to take aim and shoot at the player, but don't forget everything you've learned. Their height advantage over you will only last as long as their base is still standing, so look for weak points and open fire on those instead. It will reduce their base—and their health—to zero!

WHEN DEFENDING YOUR SIMPLE FORT

Simple forts may have their limitations, but they do the basic things well. Avoid making a tall fort so that the fall won't eliminate you if it's destroyed. If someone damages the building, replace walls as they're ruined. Their ammo won't last forever.

WHEN YOU HEAR AN INCOMING ROCKET

You'll hear an incoming rocket before it's too late, but you'll need to act fast to survive! Listen carefully to sense the rocket's direction, then throw up some walls between it and you! It takes ages to reload a rocket launcher, so find the shooter before they fire again.

6

7

WHEN YOUR OPPONENT IS A FAST BUILDER

We've encouraged you to practice building as much as possible. You can always spot someone who's put the time in, as they're lightning fast when it comes to construction. However, someone concentrating on their building won't be paying attention to you. Use this time to leg it **ASAP**!

WHEN YOU NEED TO RETREAT

As you traverse the Battle Royale map you should always remember where you've passed. How far back was the nearest settlement? Knowing this information should decide your next move. Build some walls and ramps and stay behind them, or build them to disguise your run to a safe house.

8

9

WHEN SOMEONE IS RAMP RUSHING YOU

Players love rushing up ramps to reach enemy bases, and we aren't surprised—we've already highlighted this as a great technique. But how do you defend against it? The key is in watching their path ... keep an eye on it until you can read it, then build floors or ramps outwards to block them!

WHEN YOU GET TANGLED UP IN A BASE

No matter how you approach breaching an enemy base, there's a very real chance that you'll get lost inside it. If you lose sight of your opponent and can't find a quick exit, the temptation is to blast to freedom through the walls. But be warned: they could have lost track of where you are, and firing some rounds will only lead them back to you!

10

PREPARING FOR VICTORY

Nearly there! Claiming a Victory Royale in *Fortnite* is a truly awesome experience, but you need a solid gameplan before taking to the battlefield. Establish your fighting form to figure out what works best for you.

FIND YOUR FORTNITE

LIVE LIFE ON THE EDGE

The desire to get cracking can make you a little trigger-happy and eager to leave the Battle Bus the instant the countdown has finished. Stick with it and land on the outskirts instead. Not only will it give you time to thank the driver (a funky Season 5 addition) but you'll also find fewer players have joined you. Load up on supplies without unnecessary pressure.

CELEBRATE STARTER STATUS

No one can be an expert overnight, so once you've hit the deck and suitably stocked up, don't rush and rotate to the next town straight away. Use a less-popular location to familiarize yourself with the controls. It's one of the rare occasions where firing a gun won't put fellow players on red alert.

MIX IT UP

Fortnite is one giant map of exploration, so go and explore! The game's top pros know every location inside out, which means they're better equipped when seeking loot and reaching the endgame. With every season introducing new quirks, you want to be one step ahead of the rest.

KEEP YOUR EYES ON THE PRIZE

This sounds simple, but regularly refer to the map to make sure you're either close to the safe circle or aware of the route once the storm draws near. Players can often be so preoccupied with building, looting, and planning attacks that they lose sight of their surroundings. Sometimes it's too late!

SAMPLE YOUR STRATEGY

SHOOTING VS. BUILDING

Let's get this straight—one isn't any better than the other in *Fortnite*. You need to be equally good at both as they ultimately go hand-in-hand; you build to protect and shoot, you shoot to eliminate. Find a quiet area of the map to hone your skills by creating huge structures and firing off rounds with abandon.

DID YOU KNOW?

*Wailing Woods is now a well-known haven for **NOOBS** to practice, so look out for others doing the same. You might just manage a cheeky elimination in the process. Sweet!*

SOLO, DUOS, AND SQUADS

Playing on your own can be lonely at the beginning, so rope in friends to help you along the way. You might find it more enjoyable to sit back as a sniper while your pals go on the offensive or to build around an injured cohort who needs time to heal. Teamwork really enhances the game and communicating over headsets can ramp up the banter—and the rivalry.

SEE HOW OTHERS DO IT

Being eliminated can be a blessing in disguise. On one hand, you'll know what not to do next time (so you'll improve with every game) and on the other, it gives you an opportunity to see how the rest of the game plays out. Before heading back to the Lobby, take note of fellow players and what they do to survive. You could bag even more useful tips!

READY FOR ROYALE!

SCOPE YOUR SURROUNDINGS

Even if you think you've landed in a secluded area, **NEVER** presume you're on your own. It's possible someone may have spotted you landing and set up position to take you out after you've collected loot. Listen for footsteps and the sound of gunshots, then start to make your move.

BUILD UP MATERIALS

Be it wood, brick, or metal, you'll need materials from the outset. Jumping around is fine, but opponents (especially in big cities) will eventually pick you off if you've got nothing else. Remember: building is key for both defensive and offensive strategies. Ramp up, then rush!

PICK YOUR BATTLES

Early in the game, try not to be too fixated on a player you've exchanged shots with. Sometimes the rush isn't worth the fight, especially if there's a chance they're better equipped than you. Moving on and leaving an enemy hanging is hugely satisfying if they're sitting in a house waiting for you.

LOOT WISELY

It's easy to get carried away with scooping up a shiny new arsenal, but over-looting early isn't necessary. Grab basic essentials (enough materials to build, one to two weapons and a healing option) and proceed. You'll find plenty more elsewhere, mostly when you eliminate enemies. Bonus!

ARRANGE YOUR INVENTORY

Quickly switch between weapons in the heat of battle. Stick to a shotgun, SMG, and sniper rifle, then experiment with different combos. Regularly reload (even after one fire—it can be the difference between an elimination or being eliminated) and **NEVER** run rogue with a pickaxe.

BITE THE BULLET

While playing with caution is key, you'll eventually be itching to test yourself in true 1v1 combat. Just remember that patience is a key component for success in *Fortnite*; sometimes you'll be camped for a good five minutes before drawing an enemy out. Don't be the first to buckle!

10 FOR 10

So that's pretty much all you need to know from Battle Bus to endgame. Excited? Now just heed these final 10 tips for, er, the final 10 hits.

RESOURCE RIGHT! Harvest as you go, but don't ruin possible shelters.

LEAVE NO TRAIL! Keep things tidy so your foes can't follow you.

HIT THE HEAD! Save ammo and claim an instant kill with one hit.

FOUNDATIONS! Destroy bases from the bottom to cause fall damage.

GO HIGH! Clear vision and more cover are important at the end.

SHOOT SAVVY! Don't give up your spot if you don't have a clean shot.

STUDY THE STORM! Hide near the storm's edge and take out your foes.

LURK! Let others battle and pick off the winner before they can heal.

BUILD BRAVE! Structures are a clue. Enemies will know you're close.

FOCUS! Keep your eyes on the screen. Little details can be the difference between Victory Royale or an early elimination.

DOS AND DON'TS

There you have it! We've looted you up with the all the essential info you need to become a Battle Royale superstar. Digest everything you've read and find the best ways to make our tips work in your favor. Good luck!

GETTING STARTED

 DO familiarize yourself with all the game's key components. Learn **ALL** the controls (set hotkeys for specific tools on PC and Mac) and make the Lobby your home. Progress begins here.

 DON'T rush into things. *Fortnite* isn't going anywhere, so you'll only hinder your progress if you jump in blind without knowing how to land, build, loot, harvest … the list goes on.

LEARNING THE ROPES

DO practice, practice, practice. As it stands, *Fortnite* doesn't have a permanent training mode, so find a remote spot and start crafting.

 DON'T stay secluded for too long. Hanging out can keep you in the game, but sooner or later you'll need to fight–and that means encountering enemies.

MAPS AND LANDING

 DO check out the entire map. Naturally, you'll have favorite locations, but it doesn't hurt to test out some new spots when you're more confident. Tilted Towers, here we come!

 DON'T expect chests to be in the same place every time you land. While *Fortnite* does keep things similar, it's still completely random from the Battle Bus route to the placement of loot.

BUILDING

DO become a master builder. Whether you're taking cover to heal, prepping to peek on an enemy or stemming a fall from high ground, there's no end to the awesome creations you can edit once you've mastered the art.

 DON'T disregard its importance in the game. Learning to maneuver and shoot is decent, but if you can't back it up with builds, the endgame will be very short.

LOOTING AND ITEMS

 DO stay fully stocked at all times. Harvest materials whenever you get a safe opportunity and remember, you can find items absolutely anywhere on the map. Look out for those llamas!

 DON'T overload your inventory. You want to transition swiftly between each item and know the order. If you've got shield potions, drink them and create space.

WEAPONS

 DO choose whatever suits your game. The ideal scenario is to have weapons ranging from short to long distance, but not if you're not confident using one. There's no correct way in *Fortnite*—you play the game **YOUR** way.

 DON'T forget to regularly reload. If you think it's unnecessary, consider a scenario where you're taken down while changing rounds. Annoying, isn't it?

COMBAT AND MOVEMENT

 DO stay on the move. It can be exhausting to be constantly on the go, but keeping active—be it sprinting through fields or peeking over a rock—keeps you in the game.

 DON'T stay out in the open for too long. If you're on the ground, you're exposed to whoever might be above you. For the last time in this book: **GET TO HIGH GROUND**!

GAMEPLAY

 DO take a break. Your eyes, hands and brain will be fried after a mammoth session. *Fortnite* fatigue is a thing—no matter how much you love playing the game! Chill, the wins will come.

 DON'T give up. Rome wasn't built in a day—and neither was that epic metal structure some dude used to eliminate you earlier on. Patiently persist and, eventually, you'll reap the rewards.

A FINAL WORD FROM US ...

We hope you have enjoyed all we've thrown at you. We'd love to say everyone who buys this book will be consistently getting Victory Royales by the time they reach this page. But this book isn't a quick fix. Instead, it's a long-term plan that **WILL** get you wins, but **ONLY** if you put in the time to learn the game properly.

Now you've reached this point in the book, go back to the start. Take each skill we've taught you and **PRACTICE**. Have the book open as you play. Learn locations, know where to find chests, practice with all the weapons, focus on build battles with friends or pushing players on the outskirts. Do every skill ten times. Then do it again.

Forget about winning: get good, and those Victory Royales **WILL** come!

SAFETY TIPS

YOUNGER FANS' GUIDE

Spending time online is great fun. As *Fortnite* might be your first experience of digital socializing, here are a few simple rules to help you stay safe and keep the internet an awesome place to spend time:
• Never give out your real name—don't use it as your username.
• Never give out any of your personal details.
• Never tell anybody which school you go to or how old you are.
• Never tell anybody your password, except a parent or guardian.
• Before registering with *Fortnite*, ask a parent or guardian for permission.
• Take regular breaks, as well as playing with parents nearby, or in shared family rooms.
• Always tell a parent or guardian if something is worrying you.

> **NOTE**
> *Fortnite: Battle Royale* is ESRB rated T

PARENTS' GUIDE

ONLINE CHAT

In *Fortnite*, there is live, unmoderated voice and on-screen text chat between users. At the time of writing, turning off text chat isn't possible. You can, however, turn off voice chat:
• Open the Settings menu in the top right of the main *Fortnite* page, then the cog icon. Choose the Audio tab at the top of the screen. From there, you can adjust several audio features, including voice chat. Turn the setting from "on" to "off" by tapping the arrows.
• On consoles, you are also able to disable voice chat completely in the Parental Controls, or you can set it so your child can only chat with users who have previously been added as friends. It's important to stress to your child that they shouldn't add anyone as a friend they don't know in real life. To find these controls, see opposite about in-game purchases.

SOCIAL MEDIA SCAMS

There are many accounts on Facebook and Twitter that claim to give away free V-Bucks, which will be transferred to their account. Be skeptical – it's important to check the authenticity of these accounts and offers before giving away personal information.

SOUND

Fortnite is a game where sound is crucial. Players will often wear headphones, meaning parents won't be able to hear what is being said by strangers. Set up your console or computer to have sound coming from the TV as well as the headset so you can hear what other players are saying to your child.

REPORTING PLAYERS

If you see or hear a player being abusive, you can easily report them.
• Open the Settings menu in the main *Fortnite* page. Select the Feedback option, which allows you to report bugs, send comments or report players.
• After you've been eliminated from a game, you're also given an option to report a player by holding down the corresponding button at the bottom of the screen.

SCREEN TIME

Taking regular breaks is important. Set play sessions by using a timer. However, *Fortnite* games can last up to 20 minutes and if your child finishes playing in the middle of a round, they'll leave their teammates a person short and lose any points they've earned. So, it is advisable to give an advanced warning for stopping play.

IN-GAME PURCHASES

Fortnite does offer the ability to make in-game purchases such as new clothes, dances (emotes), and equipment, but they're not required to play the game. They also don't improve a player's performance.

To set up parental controls:
• For PlayStation 4, you can create special child accounts that can be linked to your adult account, which lets you set monthly spending limits. Log into your main PS4 account. Go to Settings > Parental Controls > Family Management. Choose Add Family Member > Create User, and then enter your child's name and date of birth. You can set up specific parental controls.

• For Xbox One, you can create a special passcode to verify purchases. Go to Settings > All Settings > Accounts > Sign-in. Then choose Change My Sign-In & Security Preferences, and scroll right to Customize. Scroll right again and select Ask For My Passkey To Make Purchases, and choose Passkey Required. Simply pick a PIN your child won't guess.

• For PC and Mac, go into the account settings of your child's Epic Games account. Once in there, make sure there aren't any card details or linked PayPal accounts. You can easily remove them if they are there.

• For iPhone and iPad, whenever you make a purchase, you'll always have to verify it with either a password, the Touch ID fingerprint scanner or Face ID. But some iPhones are set up so that you only have to enter a password every 15 minutes. To stop this, go to Settings > Your Name > iTunes & App Store. Underneath you'll see a Password Settings Section. Go to Purchases And In-App Purchases, and choose Always Require. If your child knows your iPhone password, you can set up a second PIN for purchases. Go to Settings > General > Restrictions, then press Enable Restrictions. Choose a new four-digit passcode for In-App Purchases.